The Mice jum
turned to hi
and woolly universe of ours, there's only three things you can count on."

Throttle pointed to his head. "Your brains..."

He clapped his friends on their broad shoulders. "...Your bros..."

Throttle stepped on the bike's kickstart and revved the engine. "...And your bike!"

As Vinnie and Modo started up their motorcycles, Throttle shouted, "It's time to rock 'n' ride!"

Ride along with Throttle, Vinnie, and Modo on all the Biker Mice adventures!

#1 Rock 'n' Ride!
#2 Hands off My Bike!

Rock 'n' Ride!
by Justine Korman

Bullseye Books
Random House New York

A BULLSEYE BOOK PUBLISHED BY RANDOM HOUSE, INC.

Copyright © 1994 by Brentwood Television Funnies, Inc. All rights reserved under International and Pan-American Copyright Conventions. Published in the United States by Random House, Inc., New York, and simultaneously in Canada by Random House of Canada Limited, Toronto. BIKER MICE FROM MARS and all other character names and the distinct likeness thereof are the trademarks and copyrights of Brentwood Television Funnies, Inc., and are used with permission.

Library of Congress Catalog Card Number: 94-67431
ISBN: 0-679-86859-3
RL: 2.6

Manufactured in the United States of America 10 9 8 7 6 5 4 3 2 1

Rock 'n' Ride!

Out of Left Field

"This is living!" Modo said. The big gray Mouse flexed his bionic arm and squeezed the top off a can of Martian root beer. "Now all we need are some tunes."

He leaned back in his chair and looked over at his two friends, Throttle and Vinnie.

"Relax. I'm working on it," said Vinnie as he turned the dials on their long-distance scanner. Vinnie's fur was all white. A metal plate covered one side of his face.

Throttle, the leader of the group, lifted his sunglasses to read the instrument panel. The tan Mouse sat between Modo and Vinnie, piloting their cycladrone cruiser. "We're approaching Earth," he said. "Try tuning in on their radio signals."

"Gotcha, sweetheart," said Vinnie.

Suddenly, the sounds of an electric guitar poured through the speakers. All three Mice pricked up their large ears to listen.

With a loud crash of chords, the song ended, and a DJ's voice broke in. "Sweet Georgie Brown with the outlaw sounds of Guns and Noses. Hold on to your ears, because next we're going to hear—"

"All right!" yelled Vinnie. He looked over at his bros. "Any planet with heavy metal music must have intelligent life."

Suddenly there was a crash that wasn't from the music. The vidscreen lit up with large red letters:

DAMAGE ALERT

"We've been hit!" Throttle said.

"No kidding!" Vinnie said from the floor.

The blast had knocked him clean out of his seat.

The screen changed, displaying:

STABILIZER FAILURE

UNABLE TO REPAIR

Modo's root beer bounced across the floor. "What's going on?" he asked.

Throttle cleared the damage report from the vidscreen and switched to the cycladrone's outboard cameras. The tan fur on the back of his neck stood on end. A sharklike Plutarkian destroyer was right on their tail.

"I don't know how they tracked us, but they did," Throttle said grimly. "Helmets!" he shouted. "The next hit might breach the hull."

The Mice put on helmets shaped to fit over their big, round ears.

"Plutarkians!" Modo sniffed the air. "I can almost smell them from here." He closed his faceplate.

Vinnie patted the gun controls next to his seat. "What do you say we fry the fins off those stinkfaces?"

Kaboom! The cruiser was rocked by another particle beam.

"Do it!" Throttle commanded.

Vinnie aimed the vaporizer gun at the Plutarkian destroyer. "One fishface barbecue coming up!" he cried.

But before the cocky Mouse could fire, the Plutarkians shot the gun right out of his paws.

"Oh, man..." Vinnie groaned.

"It works better if you shoot before the weapon flies out the door," Throttle said. Sparks flew off the control panel as he tried to keep the damaged ship in one piece.

"Yeah, well, timing's everything," Vinnie said.

"So what're we going to do?" Modo demanded.

Throttle bounced in his seat as another shot rocked the ship. "That's easy. The ship's been captured by Earth's gravity. We're going down!"

"We're going to crash?" Vinnie asked.

"Call it a forced landing," Throttle said.

"I'm homing in on that radio signal. Sweet Georgie Brown's about to get three new local fans."

In seconds, the cruiser reached Earth's atmosphere. Friction cooked the hull as they hurtled toward the surface.

Throttle pulled back on the altitude control lever as hard as he could. The lever broke off in his paws. He tossed it aside in disgust. "I knew I should have gone for the power steering."

Vinnie's ears quivered. He could hear the roar as flames surrounded the cruiser. Most Mice, or men, would feel afraid. But Vinnie just felt excited! "Whoa! Danger and destruction! What a rush!"

"Modo! Get 'em ready to eject," Throttle commanded.

The big Mouse punched switches on the cruiser's control panel. A floor hatch slid open. A metal box rose from the ship's cargo bay. Inside were three very special vehicles—from the chrome handlebars to the atomic spacetread tires, they were the coolest, fastest, most powerful motorcycles this side of the Milky Way!

The Mice jumped onto their bikes. Throttle turned to his friends. "Guys, in this wild and woolly universe of ours, there's only three things you can count on."

Throttle pointed to his head. "Your brains…"

He clapped his friends on their broad shoulders. "…Your bros…"

Throttle stepped on the bike's kickstart and revved the engine. "…And your bike!"

As Vinnie and Modo started up their motorcycles, Throttle shouted, "It's time to rock 'n' ride!"

Peanuts! Hot Dogs!

"Boooo!" Jim hooted as another Nubs batter struck out.

"Oh man, this is too much," said Jim's friend, Tom. The boys didn't often get to attend a night game at Quigley Field. But the game was so dull, they were blowing all their money on snacks.

"And as Chicago takes the field..." the announcer said through a yawn. Suddenly he blurted, "Holy Toledo! What in blazes is that?"

The boys looked up and saw something big and metallic streak across the dark sky. Bright orange flames trailed behind it like streamers on a kite.

"Whoa! Plane crash!" Tom gasped.

"No way," said Jim. "That's got to be a UFO!"

A side hatch blew off the burning ship, and three objects shot out of the opening. An instant later, the spaceship smashed into the scoreboard, showering sparks and shattered glass over the stadium.

Panic seized the fans. Some sat frozen to their seats in fear. Others ran for the exits.

Tom stared up at the mysterious shapes descending to the field. "Those are motorcycles!" he said.

Jim nodded. "Check out the guys riding them."

The three bikes bounced on the pitcher's mound and skidded to a stop. Dirt sprayed up around three sets of atomic spacetread tires.

The helmeted riders lifted shiny faceplates. Their purring choppers were so slick they looked fast even when they were sitting still.

The biggest rider cleared his throat, glanced over at his friends, and said, "We're the Biker Mice from Mars. We come in peace."

The rider next to him laughed. The boys could see that half of his face was covered by a metal plate. Whoever he was, he had serious attitude. "Yeah," he said. "Um...take us to your leader."

"Wow," Jim said. "These guys really are aliens!"

"Too cool," said Tom.

The leader of the group saluted the crowd and said, "Didn't mean to cause any trouble, citizens."

Then he turned to his friends. "Okay, boys, kick it!"

The engines roared. Flames burst from chrome tailpipes. The bikes reared up on their back wheels and shot up the stairways between the bleachers.

Tom and Jim spun around to watch the nearest rider go up the steps.

"Awesome bikes!" said Tom.

Jim looked at his friend. "Did those guys have tails?"

Vinnie roared through the cement access tunnel behind the stands. He stopped for a moment to check his bike. The machine seemed sluggish.

He realized why: Earth's gravity was stronger than that of Mars. The air was thicker, too. The Mouse sniffed the dense air through his open helmet. Something smelled tasty.

As Vinnie neared the source of the savory smell, he saw a teenage Earthling holding a crowbar. "Just gimme your money! Now!" the young Earthling said.

Vinnie watched a frightened Earthman reach into the pocket of his white apron. The human stood behind a cart topped with a bright umbrella that said HOT DOGS.

What's a 'hot dog'? Vinnie wondered. But there was no time to buy a Mars-Earth dictionary. And he didn't need one to know that the Earthman was in trouble!

Vinnie knew what it felt like to have a bully steal what was yours. After all, the stinking Plutarkians had taken his whole planet! He gunned his engine and rode straight for the punk.

Surprised, the punk stumbled out of the way. He fell hard, and the crowbar flipped out of his hand.

Vinnie caught the bar in midair and spun his bike to a screeching halt. The white Mouse grinned and twirled the crowbar on his fingers. Being a hero was a gas!

"Hey, sweetheart. You didn't really plan on hurting anyone with this thing, did ya?" Vinnie asked.

The frightened punk scrambled to his feet. "Ah...no, sir."

"Good. Then if you don't mind..." Vinnie tossed the metal bar into the air, then flipped a switch on his bike. A cannon popped up and fired a laser beam, instantly vaporizing the crowbar.

"Bingo!" Vinnie grinned.

The punk started to back away. "Uh, I gotta go now. I think I hear my mom calling me," he mumbled. Then he turned and ran.

Vinnie turned back to the hot dog vendor. "Nice trick, eh, citizen?"

"Gee...thanks, mister," the vendor said. Then he lifted a hatch on his cart and pulled something out of the steam.

It was a long, reddish tube. The Earthman placed it in the crevice of a bun. Vinnie watched him squirt a line of yellow goo down the steaming tube. "Here," he said. "Have a dog."

Vinnie took the offering. The hot dog felt warm in his paw. Up close, the smell was even more delicious. Then he took his first bite.

Wow! Spicy, warm, bursting with flavor. Vinnie gulped down the delicious new food.

"So this is a hot dog!" Vinnie exclaimed around a mouthful of the tasty sausage. He had to give the little blue planet credit. Heavy metal and hot dogs—two points for

Earth. Maybe crashing here wouldn't be so bad after all!

The Pitch Is Good!

Throttle and Modo rode toward each other across the top of the stadium wall.

"You see any way down?" Modo asked.

Throttle shrugged his shoulders. "The usual."

With a rev of their bikes' super-engines, the Mice leaped off the concrete wall. Vinnie joined them in midair. As they touched down in the parking lot, Throttle yelled, "Let's roll!"

Vinnie scanned the streets as they rode. He was very disappointed. Where were the swank buildings, the night life, the beautiful babes?

The scene that blurred past his bike looked more like deserted ruins than one of Earth's major cities. The few standing buildings were all boarded up. The Biker Mice found themselves jumping over huge craters that pockmarked the road.

Modo's stomach lurched. The scarred and empty streets reminded him of Mars during the early days of the Plutarkian invasion, before the war broke out in earnest.

Throttle was also confused by the strange appearance of the Earth city. But he was more upset by the sound of his bike. "Hold 'em up," he said into his helmet radio.

All three supercycles screeched to a halt. "Listen to this," Throttle said. He revved his engine. The Mice heard a rattling sound.

"Busted gyro?" Vinnie asked.

Throttle nodded. "Earth gravity must've strained it to the breaking point." He sighed. "This is not my day. First the Plutarkians attack us, instead of the other way around. Then we crash the cruiser. Now my bike is conking out!"

"No sweat, sweetheart. We find a cycle shop, and I'll have it fixed pronto," Vinnie said. He was the best mechanic of the three.

Modo was doubtful. "I don't know. We've been on these streets for miles, and I haven't seen a repair pit yet."

"But look on the bright side," Vinnie replied.

"What bright side?" Throttle asked.

Vinnie pointed across the street. "*That* bright side!"

Only then did Throttle and Modo see the small building standing alone in a block of ruins. The sign above its wide sliding door showed a picture of a motorcycle under the words THE LAST CHANCE GARAGE.

"I'll scope it out," Vinnie said.

As he rode toward the building, his ears, evolved for the thin Martian atmosphere, picked up the sound of a high voice yelling.

16

"Greasepit, you can tell your slimy boss I don't care how much money he has! The Last Chance Garage is not for sale!"

Vinnie heard a lower voice say, "You is not being wise, lady. Mr. Limburger wants this land. And what Lawrence Limburger wants, Lawrence Limburger gets."

There was a scuffle. Then Vinnie heard the high voice exclaim, "Ouch!"

Greasepit growled, "Maybe now you'll see Mr. Limburger's offer in a new light!"

Vinnie snarled. It was time to quit listening and start acting! He rode into the garage and hopped off his bike.

He saw a big thug dripping with black grease, standing over a pretty young Earthwoman. She was sprawled in an oily puddle on the garage floor.

Vinnie flexed his muscles and growled, "Say there, citizen. Why don't you leave the lady alone?"

"Who's gonna make me?" Greasepit challenged.

Vinnie grinned. "*I'm* gonna make you,"

he said. He grabbed an engine hoist chain and swung toward the thug. He winked at the astonished woman. "Lookin' good, eh, sweetheart?"

But before Vinnie could land a punch, he landed on the floor and slipped in a puddle of Greasepit's gunk. "Oh man!" Vinnie shrieked as he slid into the wall.

"Aw, what's the matter?" the thug sneered. "The widdle bitty biker hurt himself? Get up and fight. What are you, anyway, a man or a mouse?"

Just then, Throttle and Modo crashed through the windows. The two Biker Mice removed their helmets to reveal their mouse ears and Martian antennae.

"Mouse," Modo said.

"You got a problem with that?" Throttle asked.

Greasepit and the garage owner gaped in amazement.

"This is one crummy place you got here. It's crawling with rats!" Greasepit complained.

Modo's good eye blazed red with fury.

"Rat? My mama didn't raise no stinking rat!"

Modo raised his bionic arm, and a laser gun popped out. He aimed at the oily villain. "Let's take this wrench-head down!"

Throttle twirled his tail around Greasepit's feet. Modo aimed the laser on his arm at the tire rack above the thug's head. Greasepit looked up just in time to see the laser cut through the rack supports.

Rubber rained down on him. In seconds, Greasepit was up to his neck in tires, looking like a pack of grease-flavored Life Savers. Throttle gave a tug with his tail, and Greasepit toppled to the ground.

Vinnie grinned. "Time to roll, sweetheart." With a hard kick, he sent Greasepit rolling out the door.

Greasepit's voice grew faint as he spun out of sight. "Mr. Limburger ain't gonna like thiiiiiiiis!"

The Home Team

Vinnie wiped grease off his foot. "Talk about your slippery customers!"

Throttle turned to the garage owner. "You okay, ma'am?"

Charley opened her mouth, but no sound came out. She had lived in Chicago all her life and had seen a lot of weird-looking guys. But this beat all!

She stared at the three bikers dressed in studded jeans and leather boots. If she hadn't known better, she'd say they were mice. But they were taller than she was!

She looked around the familiar garage. Everything else looked normal. But then there were these guys covered in fur, with big buck teeth, ears the size of dinner plates, long swirling tails, and—to top it off—antennae!

Charley backed away and waved a wrench with shaking hands. "Don't you come any closer, you...you..."

"Mice, ma'am. We're mice. We just came in to get my bike fixed," Throttle said. Her high voice was grating, but he was starting to get used to Earth's noises.

"Yeah, we're the good guys," Modo added.

"Talk about no appreciation!" Vinnie complained.

"I don't believe this," Charley muttered. "I've just been saved by a bunch of giant gerbils."

"Mice," Throttle repeated gently. He felt sorry for the Earthwoman. He knew they must look strange to her.

"You were expecting turtles, maybe?" Vinnie asked.

Charley put down the wrench and cautiously touched Vinnie.

"Mice…with…antennae…and…bike clothes…and motorcycles," Charley said.

"Don't forget your basic studly bods," Vinnie boasted, flexing his muscles.

Charley snorted. "I've seen better."

"Maybe, but not with this much charm." Vinnie wiggled his eyebrows.

Charley ignored him. "Where on Earth did you guys come from?"

"Mars," Modo said.

"Mars? Oh, right. Mars."

Throttle sighed. "Look, it's a long story. Our planet was invaded by a race of smelly stinkfaces called Plutarkians."

The tan Mouse leaned toward Charley. His antennae glowed. "Why don't you let me show you?" he said softly. He touched his antennae to Charley's forehead.

She almost backed away, but the antennae felt like gentle fingers. And then they tingled against her skin.

Suddenly, the familiar garage faded from view. Charley found herself looking at a vast red desert. Huge machines ripped down odd-looking buildings and dug craters in the rusty-red soil. Dark, heavy clouds danced in the purple sky. Charley realized she was seeing Mars!

"The Plutarkians wanted our land." Throttle's voice accompanied the images filling Charley's mind. "It seems they wasted all their own natural resources, so they go around strip-mining the cosmos."

"They blew up your planet?" Charley asked.

Modo answered. "Nah. They bought up our planet. Tore the place apart and dug up the land to ship back to Plutark. By the time we realized it was an invasion, it was too late."

Charley saw an army moving across the red dust. She realized they were giant Mice, like her strange visitors. The Martian Mice were fighting against bizarre blue aliens.

Those must be Plutarkians, Charley realized. She flinched in horror. The scaly creatures stood on two legs like people, but their huge heads had the gills and fins of fish.

"The cavemouse population fought back, but most of us were wiped out," Throttle's voice went on.

Charley recognized the three Mice leading the desperate rebels. One was tan, another white, a third gray. These Mice!

The view changed. There were no more warring Mice, only a wasteland dotted with craters.

"There were just too many of the stinkfishes. We couldn't win," Vinnie said. His voice was full of sadness.

Then the tingling antennae broke contact.

Charley thought for a moment. Finally, she said, "I think you guys should see something."

Charley pushed the button to lift the garage door. Outside were several huge digging machines.

"Those look like Plutarkian earthmovers!" Vinnie said.

Charley's voice was urgent. "Not long ago, this real estate developer came here from out of the blue and started buying up the city."

"Just like on Mars," Modo said, looking at Throttle.

"His name is Lawrence Limburger," Charley said. "He's already bought up half the town. But instead of building, all he does is tear down."

Throttle nodded. "Could be this Limburger clown is a stinkfish in disguise."

Modo scanned the horizon. "Those are Plutarkian diggers, all right."

Throttle shook his head sadly. "That explains the ship that shot us down. The Plutarkians didn't follow us. From the look of things, they've been on Earth for quite a while."

Charley shivered. "What're we going to do?"

"Don't worry, sweetheart," Vinnie said.

He pumped his fist. "We're the baddest bros in the galaxy."

Then he turned to Throttle and Modo. "Looks like we don't have to wait till we get to Plutark. We can have us that stinking fish fry right here on Earth!"

5
Foul

Lawrence Limburger plucked a worm out of the crystal bowl on his desk. He dangled it over his mouth, then popped it between his thick lips with a loud smack.

From his deluxe office atop Limburger Tower, the Plutarkian looked down at the ruined city of Chicago and chuckled. "Ah, Chicago," he purred. "Soon all of your precious soil will be mine."

Limburger looked like any normal bazillionaire. He wore an expensive purple suit and fancy white gloves. But to look like a human, he had to wear a heavy rubber mask. And that made him sweat. A lot.

The air conditioners and fans were helpless against the Plutarkian stench. It smelled like a spoiled fish sandwich, mildewed cheese, and an old gym sock combined.

Limburger slurped another worm through his lips like a living strand of spaghetti. "Chicago, New York, Paris, Hamburg, and then I'll be promoted off this overheated planet and—"

Crash! Limburger spun around at the sound of breaking glass.

"Sorry, boss," Greasepit said. He knelt on the expensive carpet, scooping up pieces of shattered bowl and wiggling worms. A pool of black grease gathered around his knees.

Limburger sighed. Plutark, Mars, Earth, it didn't matter. Wherever you went in the galaxy, good help was always hard to find.

"Greasepit, dear boy," Limburger said.

"You're dripping on my carpet!"

"Sorry, boss," Greasepit said again. He jumped into the wastebasket to contain his oily oozings.

Limburger sighed and slumped down into his chair. "Now, as I recall, I sent you to purchase the Last Chance Garage," Limburger said. "And I believe you were then to demolish it."

"That's right, boss," Greasepit agreed.

"Then why is it still there?" Limburger bellowed.

Greasepit almost passed out as Limburger's stinky breath washed over him. He held his nose and said, "It wasn't my fault, boss, honest! These big mice…"

"Mice?" Limburger snorted. "Really, Greasepit, you don't expect me to believe…" Suddenly, Limburger was struck by a terrible notion. "Mice…on motorcycles?"

Greasepit nodded. "Yeah, boss. You know these guys?"

Limburger slammed his fist down on his desk. *"Not again!"* he screamed. "Those

Mice caused me a great deal of trouble on Mars. They're the whole reason I've been assigned to this miserable planet!"

Limburger turned to look out at the city. *What are they doing here?* he wondered. The Plutarkian's gills flapped furiously under his mask. Those Biker Mice had slipped through his fins once, but they wouldn't succeed a second time—and they certainly weren't going to interfere with his plans for Earth!

Limburger pushed a vidcom button on his desk. "Karbunkle!" he shrieked.

The screen lit up to show Dr. Karbunkle hard at work in the basement laboratory of Limburger Tower. A computer cable was plugged into one side of the scientist's oversized head. He wore black goggles and a gray lab coat. At the moment, he was attaching an arm to his three-eyed, toadlike assistant, Fred the Mutant.

Karbunkle glanced up at the monitor. "Yes, your Big Cheesiness?" he hissed.

Limburger asked, "Do you recall the

three Mice who escaped from your laboratory on Mars—the leaders of that pathetic rebellion?"

Karbunkle nodded. He dropped a fresh brain into Fred's empty head. He stapled a seam across the mutant's brow, and Fred woke up.

"Yes, most frustrating," Karbunkle said. "I had just started experimenting on them when they got away. The bionic arm on the gray Mouse was coming along nicely, as I recall. But there was so much more I could have done."

Fred waved his new arm in the air. "Hey, doc! How about four arms? Then I can clap in stereo!"

Karbunkle slammed a huge cork in Fred's mouth.

"Karbunkle! Pay attention! Those biker rebels have somehow ended up on Earth, and I want to know what you are going to do about it!"

The scientist stroked his chin thoughtfully. "Well, your Cheddar Chiefiness, if you wish to catch a mouse, you must build a better mousetrap!"

Karbunkle grabbed his latest invention, then pushed a button to activate the high-speed platform. In seconds, he was whisked up to his boss's office.

Karbunkle displayed a giant chromed mousetrap that looked as if it had been designed by Harley-Davidson.

Limburger leered. "Excellent! Now all we need is the bait!"

6

Batter Up!

"Say, you're a pretty good bike jockey," Throttle said. He watched Charley's hands move over his chopper with the speed and precision of an expert.

Vinnie gave a low whistle. He had never seen a better mechanic than this Earth-woman. She made him feel as if he didn't know a wrench from a teaspoon. "She's better than pretty good."

"There! That ought to do it," Charley

said. She grunted as she tightened a final bolt on Throttle's bike.

"Are all the mechanics around here as good as you?" Modo asked.

Charley shook her head. "I'm the best in all of Chicago!" She wiped her greasy hands on a rag. "By the way, your weapons looked like they could use a little improvement, so I put in a few extras."

Modo frowned. "Like what?"

"See for yourself," Charley said.

The big gray Mouse pushed a new button on Throttle's handlebar, and two rockets tipped with boxing gloves shot out the back—right through the closed garage door!

Modo blinked. "Slick!"

Vinnie touched the bike and exclaimed, "I like it, sweetheart. I like it!"

"Like I live for your approval," Charley said. "I'd better go out and get those before they fall into the wrong hands."

Charley stepped through the hole in the paneled door. The Mice were all tired, slowed by gravity, and a little dizzy from the oxygen-rich air. The put their feet up and cranked the sound on Charley's radio. Their favorite DJ, Sweet Georgie Brown, was playing meltdown rock 'n' roll.

Vinnie nodded his head in time to the ear-splitting thrash metal. Then he glanced at the hole in the door. "Hey, what's taking Charley-girl so long?"

An answer came from outside. "Yoo-hoo! Biker bunnies! Haul those gopher teeth of yours out here. I got something for you!"

Vinnie's ears twitched. "I know that voice! Greasepit! The slimy creep is back!"

The Mice looked out the dirt-smeared windows of the Last Chance Garage. They saw Charley, tied and gagged, sitting in the center of an elaborate metal device.

"What is that thing?" Vinnie asked.

Throttle tried to make sense of the springs and levers. "Beats me, bro. Looks like a steel octopus."

Charley whipped her head around to free her mouth from the gag. "It's a trap!" she shouted.

Greasepit clapped a greasy palm over her mouth. "Quiet, you!" he growled. Then he called to the Biker Mice. "What's the matter? Cat got your tails? Hey, that's funny!" he said, laughing at his own joke.

What's a 'cat'? Throttle wondered.

Greasepit was still laughing when the Biker Mice crashed through the windows on their superbikes. "Gee! Don't these guys ever use doors?" he wondered aloud.

The Mice screeched to a halt in front of Greasepit. "Let her go, oilbreath!" Throttle commanded.

Greasepit twirled a string around his finger. "If you bums touch me, I'll let go of this string and your friend goes..."

Greasepit snapped his fingers, *snap!*

Vinnie followed the string from Greasepit's hand to a trigger on the trap. Now he understood how the device worked! If Greasepit let go, Charley would be crushed by its sharp metal arms.

"Mr. Limburger wants to see you mousies," Greasepit said. "He says you got some jail time you didn't finish back on Mars."

Vinnie's fists itched. He wanted to pound this guy! But Charley's life was on the line. This was no time to whip tail without thinking. Vinnie looked to Throttle, who always had a plan.

"All right, bros," Throttle said. "Left flank roll number three."

Charley looked from the Biker Mice to the deadly steel arms of the trap. "Um, guys..."

"Hit it!" Throttle shouted. Three engines roared like angry tigers as the Mice headed off in different directions.

Charley watched as a long rope shot out of Throttle's bike. The grappling hook at the end snagged Greasepit by the strap of his grimy overalls. As he fell, the trigger string slipped through his fingers. With a squeal, the trap started to close.

Charley's head whipped around at the sound of a laser firing. The trap was blown to bits, but the force of the explosion sent her flying through the air.

Before she knew it, the pavement was rushing up to meet her. Charley closed her eyes and braced herself for the worst.

But instead of splatting on the road, Charley landed on something furry and firm. She opened her eyes to see Vinnie's grinning face!

"Gotcha, sweetheart," Vinnie said, spinning his bike to a halt. "Have I got class or what?"

Charley waved her hand in front of her face. "What you've got is bad breath! Have you been eating onions again?"

"Only three chili dogs with everything," Vinnie said.

Charley gave him a look.

"Hey, that's a small breakfast for a growing hero!" Vinnie rode over to meet his bros, who stood over the fallen villain.

"Three against one isn't fair!" Greasepit whined.

Throttle grabbed Greasepit's overalls. "Listen up, crude-for-brains. Tell your boss that the Biker Mice from Mars are in town, and the party's over. Got that?"

Greasepit nodded.

Vinnie chuckled. "Good. Now it's time to go."

Greasepit cringed. "Oh no…not again!"

Modo used his bionic arm to lift the big thug over his shoulder, like a pitcher ready to throw a fast ball. "Like they say at Quigley Field," he said, "batter up!"

Vinnie imitated a sports announcer. "Here's the windup…and the pitch!"

Modo hurled Greasepit toward Throttle. Throttle's punch sent him flying through the air like a home run soaring out of the park.

Greasepit's voice faded into the distance. "Mr. Limburger isn't going to like thiiiiiiis!"

7

Three Strikes

In his office, Limburger paced back and forth, wiping his face with his handkerchief. Even with the air conditioners cranked up to superhigh, he was sweating out of control.

Limburger stopped at his desk and activated Karbunkle's vidcom. Before Karbunkle could say a word, the Plutarkian shrieked, "Your mousetrap was less than a success! If you can't take care of those repulsive rodents, we're through on this planet!"

Karbunkle cringed. "But, your Supreme Cheesiness, this is only a minor setback."

Limburger pounded his fist on the desk so hard, his bowl of worms jumped. He popped a worm in his mouth and forced himself to remain calm.

"The Mouse resistance on Mars cost the Plutarkian empire a great deal," Limburger explained. "Earth is a low-priority planet. We cannot afford to spend additional resources on pest control."

Karbunkle thought a moment, then gave his boss an evil grin. "If one has rats in the attic, the only thing to do is X-Terminate them!"

The scientist stepped aside to reveal the transporter chamber. It could deliver villains from twenty-seven different dimensions, using only three gigawatts of electricity. Karbunkle flipped several switches, and the chamber crackled with voltage.

When the smoke cleared, Limburger saw a giant robot wearing a leather jacket and mirrored sunglasses. It straddled a gleaming motorcycle and had enough weapons to equip a small army.

Dr. Karbunkle grinned. "May I present the X-Terminator?"

The robot revved its bike's engine.

"Charming," Limburger said. "But can it do the job?"

"Show me the target," the robot droned. A dozen safety catches on its weapons clicked off. The motorcycle roared.

A-wooga! A-wooga! Alarms howled and red lights flashed.

Limburger punched an intercom. "Security, what's going on?"

"Sir, we're under attack by what looks like three giant mice on motorcycles!"

Limburger looked out the big picture window behind his desk. The Biker Mice looked like three comets streaking straight at him! Into the intercom, Limburger said, "Activate defenses!"

Then he turned back to Karbunkle. "Get up here and bring the robot!" he said.

"Yes, your Supreme Cheesiness," Karbunkle hissed and switched off the vidscreen.

Limburger sat down and turned to watch the Mice approaching. He rubbed his hands together. "Fools! Coming to fight me on my own turf will be the last thing you ever do."

Outside, weapon turrets popped out of the tower walls. Bullets zinged around the bikers like lead rain. The Mice desperately dodged exploding missiles.

"I don't think Limburger's exactly happy to see us," Vinnie said into his helmet radio.

Modo laughed. "He's just playing hard to get," he said.

"Cut the chatter, boys," said Throttle. "Let's take that tower."

Without another word, the Mice fired their booster rockets and rode their choppers straight up the side of the concrete-and-glass building!

As the Mice came onto the roof, three all-terrain vehicles burst from a hangar, weapons blazing.

"We've got company," said Modo.

"Spread!" Throttle commanded.

The Biker Mice swerved in three different directions. Modo reached out with his mechanical arm and knocked one driver off his vehicle.

Throttle sped toward the edge of the roof, but was cut off by the second ATV.

Glancing over his shoulder, Throttle saw the third ATV coming in right behind him for the squeeze play.

Thinking fast, Throttle hit his boosters and soared over the blockade. The third ATV couldn't stop and slammed into the other.

"Nice jump, bro," said Modo.

"That was the easy part," Throttle said. "It's time to take a bite out of the Big Cheese."

Vinnie made a face. "I hate cheese," he said.

The Mice parked their bikes at the edge of the roof and ejected their tow cables.

Ker-ash! The Mice swung through the office window on their cables. Their heavy boots thumped on the thick carpet. Throttle gazed at the expensive art and heavy drapes hanging on the walls.

Across the room was a huge picture window overlooking the city. In front of that was a large wooden desk. And sitting behind that was Lawrence Limburger himself.

He smiled. "Oh dear. Greasepit said you had a problem with doors. No matter. Here you are in the fur, so to speak. I've heard so much about you. Won't you have a seat?"

"No thanks," Throttle said. "We just stopped by to settle a few debts."

"Yeah," said Vinnie. "You know anything about that?"

"You might recognize a name," Modo said. "*Plutarkians*. Ring a bell?"

Limburger laughed. "My furry friends. Why so angry? Perhaps we could share some cheese?"

"I don't think so, Limburger," Throttle said.

"But speaking of cheese," said Vinnie, "anybody else smell something fishy?"

Modo inhaled. "Sure do, bro."

"Me too," Throttle said. He slid his tail around the desk and yanked off Limburger's mask, exposing his blue fishface. "That's the smell of sweaty Plutarkian."

Limburger flapped his gills and rolled big, googly eyes. "Oh dear," he said, sniffing his armpits. "Do I offend?"

"Definitely," Throttle said. "Take him down, Modo."

Modo started to raise his bionic arm, laser ready.

"Wait!" Limburger said, his arms up. "Someone wants to say hello to you. Someone I believe you've already met."

Limburger gestured to the side, and from behind a curtain stepped Karbunkle.

"Karbunkle!" Modo yelled. He swung his arm up and aimed the laser at the scientist.

"Oh...how nice of you to remember!" the scientist purred. He clutched a remote control in one black-gloved hand.

Modo's mechanical fist clenched. "I remember, all right. I remember how you took my arm and put this hunk of tin in its place."

"One of my better inventions," Karbunkle remarked. "And speaking of inventions, I have one you might like to meet!"

Karbunkle pressed a button on the remote control, and a wall panel slid open, exposing a secret room. "The X-Terminator!"

8

You're Out!

The massive robot powered up, rolled into the office on its cycle, and pointed huge cannons at the Mice. It spoke in a mechanical drone: *"Hasta la vista, rodents!"*

Limburger's wide lips curved into an evil grin. "Well, well. It seems it's time to say good-bye to our guests."

The Mice looked at each other. They knew they'd need their bikes to deal with this mechanical monster.

Vinnie edged back toward the window. "Hey, it's been lots of fun. We'll drop in again sometime when you're smelling...I mean, feeling better."

Limburger shook his head. His fins flopped. "Not this time."

"No, really," Modo said. "I'm afraid we have to go."

Throttle said, "If you don't mind, we'll just leave the same way we came in." He whistled, and three engines revved on the roof.

"It's been a treat, fellas. But it's time for us to rock 'n' ride!" Throttle said.

Then, to Limburger's amazement, the three Mice leaped out of the window. But instead of making the long, terrible plunge to the ground, the Martian Mice landed on their obedient choppers as the bikes raced down the building.

Limburger shrieked at the giant robot, "Exterminate them!"

Out on the open road, Throttle ducked as a laser beam whizzed past his head.

"I don't need a haircut. What gives?"

Throttle demanded with a frown.

A glance in his rearview mirror showed the giant robot gaining fast, followed by backup thugs.

"Kick it, bros!" Throttle cried.

The Martian Mice took off so fast their tailpipes spewed flames.

"You guys take Limburger's goon squad," Throttle said into his radio. "I'll handle the big fella."

Modo and Vinnie dropped back and veered off. Limburger's thugs turned to follow. Throttle looked behind him. The X-Terminator was still on his tail. Throttle smiled and gunned the engine. He had a destination in mind.

After a wild chase, Throttle turned down a road that ended in front of a toxic waste plant. Throttle spun his bike to face the robot.

"End of the road, rodent!" the X-Terminator said.

"Come and get me, tin man!" Throttle taunted.

The robot rode straight toward Throttle at full speed. Throttle held his ground until the last second. Then he gunned his chopper and flipped over backward, out of the way.

Missing its Mouse target, the X-Terminator crashed right through the front door of the toxic waste plant. It landed in a pit filled with glowing sludge. "I'll be back," the robot croaked just before the ooze covered it completely.

Throttle chuckled. "Yeah? Well, don't forget to write."

Home Plate

"It's going to take a long time to repair the ship," Throttle said sadly.

The Mice and Charley looked up at the Quigley Field scoreboard. The shattered cycladrone cruiser teetered halfway in and halfway out of the wreckage.

Even as they watched, the ship fell inside the sign.

"Typical. Just great," Throttle moaned.

"Well, if you're stuck here on Earth, this

place will make as good a hideout as any," Charley said.

She couldn't help being glad that the Biker Mice would have to stay. Chicago and Earth needed them. Besides, though she would never admit it to his furry face, Charley thought Vinnie was kind of cute.

Throttle frowned. "Here? In the scoreboard?"

Charley shrugged. "Why not? Limburger and his greasy goons would never think of looking for you here!"

"We can't afford a condo," Vinnie said.

"I've lived in worse," Modo added.

Charley led the Mice up the back stairs to the scoreboard. They walked around behind the lights and video screens.

Charley felt like a real estate agent. "Well, guys, what do you think? It's got power, big-screen TV, and a central location."

"Yeah! Right near some of the best hot dog vendors in the city!" Vinnie exclaimed.

Charley grinned. "And you'll have great seats for every game!"

Throttle sighed. "I guess we can fight the Plutarkians just as well from here as anywhere else in the galaxy."

He felt sad knowing they might not see their home planet for a very long time. But Earth was starting to grow on him. Thick air, heavy gravity, and loud noises, yes, but also hot dogs, heavy metal, and freedom.

"We'll stop those Plutarkians once and for all!" Modo said.

"Yeah!" Vinnie yelled. "The stink stops here!"

Throttle clapped his bros on the shoulders. "Mars can wait. It's not going anywhere."

Vinnie grinned. "Now that we've got the bachelor pad thing together, let's grab some chow!"

"I know a great cheese shop downtown," Charley offered.

All three Martian Mice spoke at once. "Cheese? Yecch!"

Modo was indignant. "What do you think we are, anyway?"

"Um…Mice?" Charley was confused.

Vinnie spoke up, "I was thinking maybe of a few root beers, a couple of dogs..."

With that, the Mice popped on their helmets and jumped on their bikes. Vinnie's tail swooped around Charley's waist and swept her onto the back of his bike.

Throttle called, "Okay, group. Let's rock..."

Three supercycle engines roared. The Mice and Charley shouted together, "...'n' *ride!*"

Hitch a ride with the Biker Mice in their next adventure:
#2: HANDS OFF MY BIKE!

Modo felt sick and dizzy. His fur was steaming. His boots were melting. He could barely breathe. But his first concern was his bike.

Modo staggered toward it through the thick blue goo. "Hang on, Li'l Hoss! I'm coming!"

Suddenly, Lawrence Limburger's voice boomed out from above him. "Too late, lemming!"

Limburger was hovering overhead in a helicopter! He lowered a giant clamp that fastened onto Modo's cycle.

Modo rushed forward, but fell face-first into the bubbling gunk. "My bike!"

"Not any more," Limburger said. "Now it's *mine!*"

Modo reached out toward his cycle as it rose into the sky. "*No!*"